IN SEARCH OF THE RIVER

A Spiritual Journal In Scripture And Verse

BY B. KATHLEEN FANNIN

*"You brought a vine out of Egypt;
you drove out the nations and
planted it.
You cleared the ground for it;
it took deep root and filled
the land.
The mountains were covered with
its shade,
the mighty cedars with its branches;
it sent out its branches to the sea,
and its shoots to the river."*

— Psalms 80:8-11

Fairway Press
Lima, Ohio

IN SEARCH OF THE RIVER

FIRST EDITION

7913 / ISBN 1-55673-460-3

PRINTED IN U.S.A.

To my friend and mentor

Jack

without whom many of
these thoughts might
never have been.

"Then the angel showed me the river of the water of life, bright as crystal, flowing from the throne of God and of the Lamb . . ."

—*Revelation 22:1*

Table Of Contents

"Let anyone who is thirsty come to me, and let the one who believes in me drink. As the scripture has said, 'Out of the believer's heart shall flow rivers of living water.' "

—John 7:37b-38

Preface

All of us, whether we admit it to ourselves or not, are on a spiritual journey. Too often the daily pressures of our lives leave no time for reflection, quiet meditation, silence, prayer, communion with God. Neglect of one's spiritual nature seems to be a fairly common experience in 20th century American society.

This neglect creates a deep, unnamed thirst within, an uneasiness, an emptiness which some of us never acknowledge. Some of us just learn to live with the ache.

Yet the spiritual deprivation of any one of us diminishes us all, for we are joined by the Holy Spirit to one another and to God. Each of us, in spirit, is part of every other.

Over centuries, poets have used numerous metaphors in writing about the spiritual nature of human beings and the journey we share. For me, the journey is a search for the river, the living water. Too often we are deafened to its presence by the noise of daily living. But we can, even in the midst of that noise, find those few precious daily moments to enter the pristine, untracked stillness where that deepest part of ourselves communes with our Creator. It is a place of unconditional love; it is a place in which one is never alone, for God is always there, seeking us even as we seek God; it is the place the river runs, in the Kingdom within.

The poems gathered into this book have arisen out of my own search for that river. They are thoughts which have come to me in times of quiet meditation and deep emotion, gifts from that still small voice which speaks in "sighs too deep for words."

It is my hope that some word or phrase contained herein will serve as a light along the spiritual path of every reader who comes in search of the river. Each of us must find it in our own way, in our own time.

B. Kathleen Fannin
January, 1991

"Likewise the Spirit helps us in our weakness; for we do not know how to pray as we ought, but that very Spirit intercedes with sighs too deep for words."

—*Romans 8:26*

"For everything there is a season, and a time for every matter under heaven . . ."

—*Ecclesiastes 3:1*

Introduction

The introduction to this book is really an introduction of Kathleen Fannin. Kathleen is part of a special task force at the Rickman Center in Jefferson City, Missouri, where I serve as the director. The mission of this group is to find ways to provide retreat opportunities for people to enhance their awareness of God's presence in their lives.

This book was born in some of the work Kathleen has done as a member of this task force. It is part of the "river" that was formed when the two streams of her own spiritual journey flowed together.

Through her poetry Kathleen seeks to share both her personal spiritual journey and her journey of vocational discernment. These streams have come together in this book as she shares her spiritual "river" with others through her gift of writing.

Our journeys are not alone. It is in sharing the journeys of others that we discover God's love flowing toward us.

LaDonna Hopkins
February, 1991

"In the beginning when God created the heavens and the earth, the earth was a formless void and darkness covered the face of the deep, while the spirit of God swept over the face of the waters."

—*Genesis 1:1-2*

"Then turning to the disciples, Jesus said to them privately, 'Blessed are the eyes that see what you see! For I tell you that many prophets and kings desired to see what you see, but did not see it, and to hear what you hear, but did not hear it.'"

—*Luke 10:23-24*

Vision

Adrift,
in awe of everything before me,
I sail beyond the future, past the stars;
discover there the outer shell,
the limit of what is
and what may come to be —
the final edge of space.
And beneath my gaze, the cosmos cracks.
Infinity unbound!
For one brief moment vision takes
me deep within creation's core
to look upon the face of Love
which nurtured each new soul before,
fragmented, we were sent to roam the earth.
My vision-lifted spirit soars,
exploring once again this place
where every soul begins, and comes again
to reunite with God.
But vision's gift is fleeting,
does not last.
And my soul cries out in anguish
at its age-old separation
from the vital, loving force
which gave it birth.
Adrift . . .

July 30, 1986

"For nothing is hidden that will not be disclosed, nor is anything secret that will not become known and come to light."

—Luke 8:17

"The wind blows where it chooses, and you hear the sound of it, but you do not know where it goes. So it is with everyone who is born of the Spirit."

—John 3:8

Balloons

Memories rise like bright balloons
riding mind-born winds,
carrying the many selves I've been
across eternity.

Each a part of me no longer known,
they have no strings attached to haul them down
that I might touch their secrets.

Like kaleidoscopes, they change
as recollections fade,
and I cannot remember what I knew.

But memories know . . .
and summon me to go where they have been;
to know again who it is I am;
to share their freedom, riding on the wind.

December 18, 1987

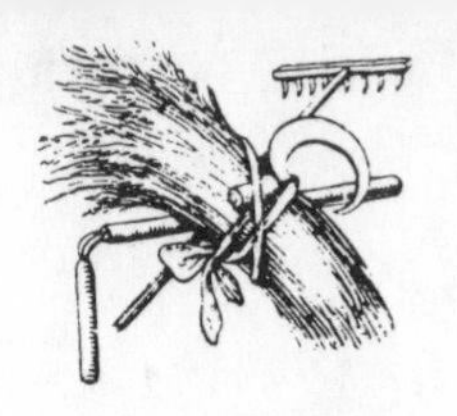

"A sower went out to sow. And as he sowed, some seeds fell on the path, and the birds came and ate them up. Other seeds fell on rocky ground, where they did not have much soil, and they sprang up quickly, since they had no depth of soil. But when the sun rose, they were scorched; and since they had no roots, they withered away. Other seeds fell among thorns, and the thorns grew up and choked them. Other seeds fell on good soil and brought forth grain, some a hundredfold, some sixty, some thirty."

—Matthew 13:3b-8

Parallels

Roots . . .
Reaching deep down
into rich dark earth,
Searching out nutrients of the soil,
A quest required to live,
A never-ending hunger for
minerals and moisture —
without which there is no future.
Where lies the future? Is it the
ultimate expectation of living things?

Roots . . .
Reaching deep down
into riches of the past,
Searching out nutrients of the soul,
A quest required to know life,
A never-ending hunger for
knowledge, understanding, truth, wisdom —
without which there is no faith.
Where lies faith? Is it the
ultimate expectation of the soul?

October 27, 1985

"Deep calls to deep
at the thunder of your cataracts;
all your waves and your billows
have gone over me."

—Psalms 42:7

"Can you find out the deep things of God? Can you find out the limit of the Almighty?"

—Job 11:7

River Talk

—for Jack

Silent river, running fast,
sending unseen demons down to die
in oceans well beyond your depths;
river do you sense
the deadly wraiths that ride
your currents swift?
Can you feel their forces strain
against deep channels you have cut
across the land?

And I wonder, silent run,
have you met God?
Or does sentience preclude
a face-to-face encounter
the like of which mankind
can only dream?
If I could liquify my soul
and merge into your torrent,
would I know?

July 28, 1987

"The floods have lifted up, O LORD,
the floods have lifted up their voice;
the floods lift up their roaring.
More majestic than the thunders of mighty waters,
more majestic than the waves of the sea,
majestic on high is the LORD!"

—Psalms 93:3-4

"Have you entered into the springs of the sea,
or walked in the recesses of the deep?"

—Job 38:16

Impressions

The ever restless sea contracts, expands,
its constant motion smoothing rumpled sands,
erasing every footprint left by those
who've walked these beaches since the tide last rose.
Compelled, the shore yields to the sea's demands.

Its pulsing waters leave faint, rippled bands
to mark their passing. As it countermands
all other imprints with its own, on flows
the ever restless sea.

My tracks alone remain upon its sands
until relentlessly the sea remands
them to oblivion, its undertows
too strong for idle footprints to oppose.
No evidence of humankind withstands
the ever restless sea.

February 28, 1989

"May those who sow in tears
reap with shouts of joy."

—Psalms 126:5

"You have turned my mourning into
dancing;
you have taken off my sackcloth
and clothed me with joy."

—Psalms 30:11

Coda

— for Jack

Joy sings —
a distant descant
sighing on the wind
high above staccato waves
of sorrow,
breaking in rhythmic requiem
upon my soul;
but when the tide is spent,
its grooves of care
washed clean within my heart,
joy remains,
to swell its song,
to lift my heart rejoicing
with resonant memories
ringing on the wind.

July 16, 1988

"Let mutual love continue. Do not neglect to show hospitality to strangers, for by doing that some have entertained angels without knowing it."

—Hebrews 13:1-2

"For I was hungry and you gave me food, I was thirsty and you gave me something to drink, I was a stranger and you welcomed me, I was naked and you gave me clothing, I was sick and you took care of me, I was in prison and you visited me."

—Matthew 25:35-36

Finale

If life has any purpose,
any point, however small,
any lasting meaning,
any consequence at all,
it is surely born of caring,
reaching out with mind and heart
to create a whole much greater
than the mere sum of its parts.

January 14, 1986

"For you were called to freedom, brothers and sisters; only do not use your freedom as an opportunity for self-indulgence, but through love become slaves to one another. For the whole law is summed up in a single commandment, 'You shall love your neighbor as yourself.' "

—Galatians 5:13-14

"When the bow is in the clouds, I will see it and remember the everlasting covenant between God and every living creature of all flesh that is on the earth."

—*Genesis 9:16*

". . . they shall beat their swords into
plowshares,
and their spears into pruning
hooks;
nation shall not lift up sword against
nation,
neither shall they learn war any
more."

—*Isaiah 2:4*

Rainbows

Perhaps life's sweetest joys are those that come
unasked, surprising us with sheer delight
and wonder, like flowers sprouting from
a rocky ledge or birds singing in the night.
The joys we don't anticipate, that spring
like bounding deer into our lives, capsize
our hearts with bliss, give birth to dreams, and bring
the misty light of rainbows to our eyes.
Of all the joys life has to give there might
be one we'd single out, to place above
all else if it should bless our lives with light,
the radiant joy of unexpected love.
What joy more precious could be ours than this:
that love would choose our lives to know its bliss?

February 1, 1989

"The wilderness and the dry land shall be glad and the desert shall rejoice, and blossom as the rose."

—Isaiah 35:1

"For as the earth brings forth its
shoots,
and as a garden causes what is
sown in it to spring up,
so the Lord GOD will cause
righteousness and praise
to spring up before the nations."

—Isaiah 61:11

Desert Rain

Spring explodes as rain
drums down on desert sands. It hears
again the music of the dance, and spears
through rain-soaked dunes with bursting buds to spill
bouquets on ozone-scented air and fill
dawn fresh with Spring.

Storm clouds race on,
rain melts away, and newborn desert sears
the hearts of people watching Spring with tears
that like the rain would vanish shed on sand.
But human flesh is clay, and clay withstands
rain drumming down
and tears on masks
we wear to hide from life, ashamed of smears
that show we heard the music once, with ears
attuned to Spring — before the years took hold,
and made us deaf to descants played by bold
rain drumming down.

New Springs, unheard,
will dance whenever desert rain appears.
And we with masks will wipe away mute tears
as raindrops drum their rhythmic beat
on desert sands, awakening dunes that greet
dawn, fresh with Spring.

February 3, 1987

"As a deer longs for flowing streams,
so my soul longs for you, O God.
My soul thirsts for God,
for the living God.
When shall I come and behold
the face of God?"

—Psalms 42:1-2

"Because your steadfast love is better
than life,
my lips will praise you.
So will I bless you as long as I live;
I will lift up my hands and call on
your name."

—Psalms 63:3-4

Yearning

Dearest Lord,
you know the hunger in my heart,
the inmost desire of my soul,
because my hunger is for you;
my yearning is to know you
as intimately as you know me.
I hear dim echoes of your voice
in the wind,
feel your faint caress
when I walk through morning mist.
I know without a doubt
you are there
and long to meet you face to face,
an encounter even imagination
cannot conceive.
I taste your being in the rain,
see the promise of your love
reflected in a rainbow,
smell the lingering sweetness
of your presence
on the petals of a rose.
God of rainbows and roses,
mists and wind,
thank you for these dim echoes,
these hints of your glory,
these partial understandings
that reach within me
and fill me with your love.
I rejoice in your being.

August 13, 1990

"Holy, holy, holy is the LORD of hosts;
the whole earth is full of his glory."

—Isaiah 6:3

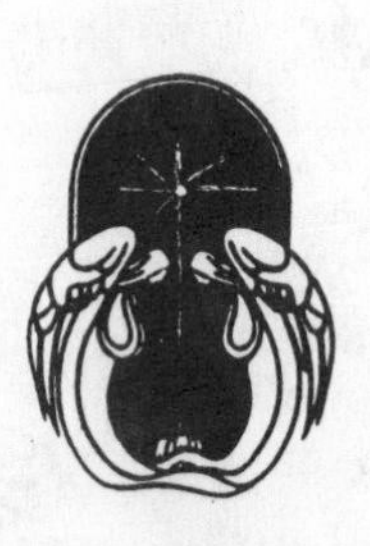

"For a child has been born for us, a son given to us . . ."

—Isaiah 9:6a

Advent

He comes in
peace . . .
. . . pristine as new-fallen snow,
. . . endless,
. . . perpetual,
. . . enduring beyond forever.

He comes in
light . . .
. . . silently shining over the earth,
. . . ethereal,
. . . ineffable,
. . . banishing darkness for all
time.

He comes in
love . . .
. . . lifting up the fallen soul,
. . . reaching,
. . . caring,
. . . sharing the human experience.

He comes in
joy . . .
. . . healing the broken spirit,
. . . softly,
. . . gently,
. . . sounding the trumpets of
eternity.

He is born . . .

November 22, 1985

" 'Let us go now to Bethlehem and see this thing that has taken place, which the Lord has made known to us.' So they went with haste and found Mary and Joseph, and the child lying in the manger."

—Luke 2:15b-16

"And the peace of God, which surpasses all understanding, will guard your hearts and your minds in Christ Jesus."

—Philippians 4:7

Mysterious Peace

Across the centuries a baby's cry
still echoes in the hearts of all who seek
an answer to the time-worn question, "Why?"
that veils our lives with palpable mystique.
As Wise Men followed starlight from above
so long ago, on hearing of His birth,
we too would find the path, and know the love
that brought the hope of peace upon the earth!
Elusive as a shadow in the sun
the Mystery yet draws us toward its light,
as we commemorate the birth of one
who came among mankind that holy night.
At Christmastide, as joy and hope increase,
may love renew our lives with Christmas peace.

December 10, 1986

"And now faith, hope, and love abide, these three; and the greatest of these is love."

—1 Corinthians 13:13

"This is my commandment, that you love one another as I have loved you."

—John 15:12

"Why?"

Then search for love, for love is all of life,
and all that brings to death significance.
Our lives, so like kaleidoscopes, are rife
with shifting possibilities that dance
in darkness if they fail to catch the light
of love to give them form and make us whole.
For only love can finally unite
our mortal flesh with our immortal soul.
The single question common to mankind
is "Why?" Why life? Why death? What mystery
created them? What makes them one? How blind
we are to love, and to eternity.
We live; we search; we may find love; we die.
But without love, we cannot answer "Why?"

November 6, 1987

". . . let us run with perseverance the race that is set before us, looking to Jesus the pioneer and perfecter of our faith, who for the sake of the joy that was set before him endured the cross . . ."

—Hebrews 12:1b-2a

"For while we live, we are always being given up to death for Jesus' sake, so that the life of Jesus may be made visible in our mortal flesh."

—2 Corinthians 4:11

For Joy

We know we cannot live unless we die,
as that which does not die can never live,
for joy can never grace the tearless eye.

And that which grows no wings can never fly.
Although life's price seems stark, prohibitive,
we know we cannot live unless we die.

Our lives are ours to treasure or deny.
But life depends on death its gift to give,
for joy can never grace the tearless eye.

And should we choose denial, fail to try,
our life slips through our fingers like a sieve.
We know we cannot live unless we die.

How could life be without death's lullaby?
We must accept that death is ours to live,
for joy can never grace the tearless eye.

We make the choice: to live, to laugh, to cry,
or come to death with untold narrative.
We know we cannot live unless we die,
for joy can never grace the tearless eye.

August 6, 1989

"When they kept on questioning him, he straightened up and said to them, 'Let anyone among you who is without sin be the first to throw a stone at her.' "

—John 8:7

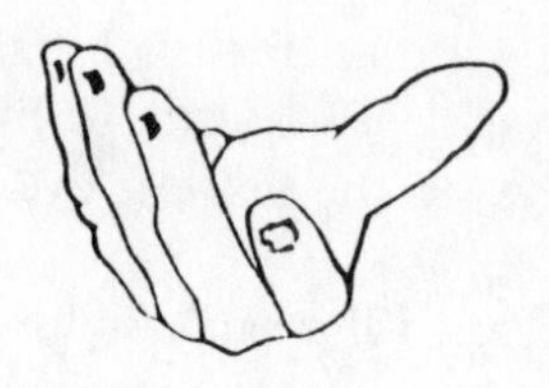

The Hurling

Hate-hurled stones await,
halted momentarily
by words I do not understand:
"Wait. The Teacher comes. Let him decide."
So, this is how it ends, here in the dust.
I sold my body only to survive,
to gain my freedom.
What I did, I did to live
and now the price is death by hate.
I dread the hurling.

A sudden hush bears witness to
the Teacher's coming.
I cower at the crunch of sand
beneath his feet.
He stops nearby and gives reply
to the question that delays my death:
"Let him who has no sin among you
cast the first stone."

Anticipating pain
too awful to imagine,
I wonder at this man who dares to speak
such challenge to a hate-filled mob.
Who is this teacher-man
whose words arrest the crowd?
I tremble in the dust, afraid to look;
afraid the first stone cast will crush my face.

But no stones come.
I hear them fall from hands which cannot hold them
bound-up as they are with sins of their own.
As I raise my eyes to meet his gaze,

my tears muddy the dust on the Teacher's feet;
my loosened hair brushes across his toes.
"Who condemns you now?" he asks in gentle tones.
I turn to look; the crowd has gone!

Naught but scattered stones remain
to mark their ever having been.
"No one's left," I whisper, choking on my words.
"Neither, then, do I condemn you, woman."
He extends his hand to draw me up
from the dirt in which I lie,
the dirt in which I thought I was to die.
"Go," he says with love. "You are forgiven.
Go and sin no more."

November 2, 1990

"And I tell you, you are Peter, and on this rock I will build my church . . ."

—Matthew 17:18a

Insight

As Spring arrives to steal across
white-crusted night where shadows dance
to music only they can hear,
melting snow streams down
from jumbled rocks, like tears
shed for something gone.
Watching from the darkness,
I think of other rocks I've known
and leaned upon for strength . . .
and through the watching, know
that even rocks, at times,
have need to cry.

January 24, 1987

"Then Peter remembered what Jesus had said: 'Before the cock crows, you will deny me three times.' And he went out and wept bitterly."

—Matthew 26:75

"Hear my cry, O God;
listen to my prayer.
From the end of the earth I call to you
when my heart is faint.
Lead me to the rock
that is higher than I."

—Psalms 61:1-2

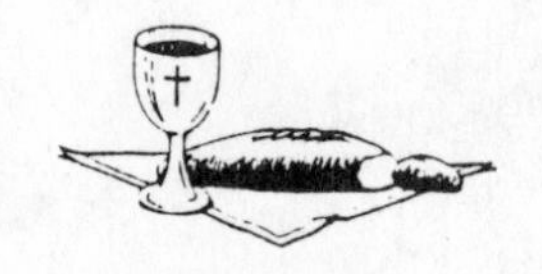

"The waters wear away the stones;
the torrents wash away the soil of
the earth . . ."

—Psalms 15:19a

Communion

Over untold years
water-washed stones
gain singular acquaintance
with the power of God,
shaping, smoothing,
wearing away
rough-hewn facades,
haunting human minds
which long to know God
as intimately as worn stones.
Held in human hands
their stream-wrought contours
mediate prayers of the people,
offering connection
to free-flowing Spirit
as created communes with Creator.

November 9, 1990

"Some of the Pharisees in the crowd said to him, 'Teacher, order your disciples to stop.' He answered, 'I tell you, if these were silent, the stones would shout out.' "

—Luke 19:39-40

"Jesus said to them, 'The light is with you for a little longer. Walk while you have the light, so that the darkness may not overtake you. If you walk in the darkness, you do not know where you are going. While you have the light, believe in the light, so that you may become children of light.' "

—John 12:35-36

"For it is the God who said, 'Let light shine out of darkness,' who has shone in our hearts to give the light of the knowledge of the glory of God in the face of Jesus Christ."

—2 Corinthians 4:6

Illumination
—for Jack

As morning wakes the slumbering shades of night,
so memory revives the sleeping shades
of friends still loved, though lost to mortal sight.
I marvel at the miracle that fades
dark night to dawn when morning flies abroad
on wings of angels; marvel at the gifts
that come with change, so gently wrought. I laud
the God who gives us memories to lift
the veil of death, as morning draws aside
the veil of night. For friends we've loved live on
in thought, their wisdom with us yet, to guide;
their joy forever ours with each new dawn.
Sweet benediction fills the morning air,
for memories that bless are living prayer.

November 14, 1988

" 'Peace I leave with you; my peace I give to you. I do not give you as the world gives. Do not let your hearts be troubled and do not let them be afraid.' "

—John 14:27

"How much better to get wisdom than gold!
To get understanding is to be chosen rather
than silver."

—Proverbs 16:16

"No one after lighting a lamp puts it in a cellar, but on the lampstand so that those who enter may see the light."

—Luke 12:33

At A Revival With The Reverend Mr. King David Cole

Silver hair,
silver robe,
rich silver words
crashing like thunder,
split the air
with deep bass sound
and break against my soul.
Suddenly shattered,
I cower afraid;
afraid of the power
that transforms words
into cannonading sound
with a life of its own,
pushing me toward
the boundary between
the things I know
and those I've never
dared to dream.
Booming, deep,
silver-bell voice,
alive with power,
hammers my fear
with questions never asked.
Do I fear the answers,
or do I fear having none?

March 22, 1988

". . . we look not at what can be seen but at what cannot be seen; for what can be seen is temporary, but what cannot be seen is eternal."

—2 Corinthians 4:18

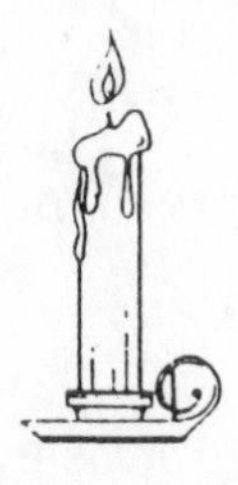

"At that same hour Jesus rejoiced in the Holy Spirit and said, 'I thank you, Father, Lord of heaven and earth, because you have hidden these things from the wise and the intelligent and have revealed them to infants; yes, Father, for such was your gracious will.' "

—Luke 10:21

Second Sight

How many opportunities
remain forever unexplored
within the unseen spaces
of our lives,
unchallenged and unchanged
because we fail to look for light
in hidden places?

As children our
imaginations burn,
melting shadows
with a single glance —
and nothing seems
impossible!
But somehow age . . .

A certain blindness comes with age;
a darkness without dreams
that leaves behind unnoticed
unborn places.
And we are left
with what our blindness sees . . .
For only in our final hour
does dark come clear
to free us from illusion.

July 27, 1987

"And she gave birth to her first born son and wrapped him in bands of swaddling cloth, and laid him in a manger, because there was no place for them in the inn."

—*Luke 2:7*

"Then an angel of the Lord stood before them, and the glory of the Lord shone around them, and they were terrified. But the angel said to them, 'Do not be afraid; for see — I am bringing you good news of great joy for all people: to you is born this day in the City of David a savior, who is the Messiah, the Lord.' "

—*Luke 2:9-11*

Crib Toy

A Christmas decoration,
probably Mexican, made from straw,
is slung beneath a brass
and crystal chandelier
as if the angels dropped it there,
by whim or accident,
while flying off to places
only angels know.
Perhaps they fashioned it from manger hay
that lay beneath a holy, newborn child;
wove this red-beribboned ring
and dangling animals that swing
so gently from its underside;
shaped this Mexican Christmas thing
to entertain His Infant Holiness
and now have dropped it here in celebration
announcing to the world that He is born.

January 3, 1990

"In the time of King Herod, after Jesus was born in Bethlehem of Judea, wise men from the East came to Jerusalem, asking, 'Where is the child who has been born King of the Jews? For we observed his star at its rising and have come to pay him homage.' "

—Matthew 2:1-2

"On entering the house, they saw the child with Mary his mother; and they knelt down and paid him homage. Then, opening their treasure chests, they offered him gifts of gold, frankincense, and myrrh."

—Matthew 2:11

Pilgrimage

Let me cross the desert with the Wise Men.
Let me travel with them from afar
following the holy light of heaven
gathered into Christ's bright natal star.

Let me sit with shepherds in their pastures
as alleluias shimmer from the heights.
Let me hear the wondrous joy of angels
proclaiming Jesus' birth that holy night.

Let me find the stable in the starlight,
enter with the shepherds and the kings,
in reverent silence kneel before the manger,
and feel the gentle brush of angel wings.

Harbored in the hush of Bethlehem
let me greet the child so long foretold.
Kneeling in the stillness let me offer
my heart beside the frankincense and gold.

January 31, 1990

"For now we see in a mirror dimly, but then we will see face to face. Now I know only in part; then I will know fully, even as I have been fully known."

—1 Corinthians 13:12

"Once Jesus was asked by the Pharisees when the kingdom of God was coming, and he answered, 'The kingdom of God is not coming with things that can be observed; nor will they say, "Look, here it is!" or "There it is!" For, in fact, the kingdom of God is within you.' "

—Luke 17:20-21

Journey Inward

Deep the river runs in silence
joining humankind to Triune God —
Creator, Spirit, Born-of-Woman
Deity within us,
living through us, yet unknown.
For noise of daily living
leaves us senseless to the silence,
the quiet, holy places seldom trod,
lost to knowing
as busy lives preclude
our search for self, our search for God.

Strangers to ourselves and to each other,
we fill our shallow lives
with emptiness and questions
for which we have no words.
Yet unnamed hunger draws us
to approach the river's mystery,
down a path of silence
we must walk alone.
And when we come at last
into the untracked stillness,
we kneel to drink
and kiss the face of God.

October 23, 1988

*"O LORD, you have searched me and
known me.
You know when I sit down and
when I rise up;
You discern my thoughts from far
away.
You search out my path and my
lying down,
and are acquainted with all my
ways."*

—Psalms 139:1-3

The Pruning

As the vinemaster knows his vineyard,
so does my God know me.
The wise vinemaster understands
the needs of every individual vine;
he knows which branches must be pruned,
despite their full, round fruit,
to glean the very best at harvest time.
So does my God know me.
But I, unlike the vine,
do not always make the best
of what remains.
The vine yields to the master's touch
and wastes not time nor energy
on what is lost.
It focuses on living,
reaching up to catch
the healing warmth of sun,
or rain's wet, soothing balm.
So do I reach toward my God,
seeking healing for my wounded soul.
At pruning time, the master vineman
makes each cut with care,
then stands aside to give the vine
both time and space to readjust
to unexpected circumstance.
So does my God wait for me.
With compassion born of intimate acquaintance,
the vinemaster nudges wandering branches
toward the trellis they must climb.
So does my God nudge me.
And, like the vine so lovingly pruned,
so nurtured with compassion,
I shall, perhaps, in time become
that which my God would have me be.

May 18, 1990

"You did not choose me but I chose you. And I appointed you to go and bear fruit, fruit that will last, so that the Father will give you whatever you ask him in my name."

—John 15:16

Remnants

Jesus, the Ragman,
collecting remnants of humanity —
the broken, the lowly,
the blind, the lame, the unclean,
those society has discarded
as unfit and useless.
Jesus, the Ragman,
weaving from the remnants
a new creation,
turning weakness into strength,
finding in humanity's diversity
new unity, new wholeness,
significance from the seemingly insignificant.

December 30, 1990

"The Spirit of the Lord is upon me,
because he has annointed me
to bring good news to the poor.
He has sent me to proclaim release
to the captives
and recovery of sight to the blind,
to let the oppressed go free,
to proclaim the year of the Lord's
favor."

—Luke 4:18-19

"For I am convinced that neither death, nor life, nor angels, nor rulers, nor things present, nor things to come, nor powers, nor height, nor depth, nor anything else in all creation, will be able to separate us from the love of God in Christ Jesus our Lord."

—Romans 8:38-39

". . . and let everyone who is thirsty
come.
Let anyone who wishes take the
water of life as a gift."

—Revelation 22:17b

Ever Green

Today I saw Him,
Christ . . .
. . . body broken,
eyes glazed, sightless,
. . . broken, bleeding, dying,
lying by the highway.
No doubt other drivers
saw a doe.
But it was Christ;
I knew.
I felt so helpless, lonely,
hopeless, knowing
there was nothing
I could do
to aid the broken doe,
the broken Christ.
I wept, and watched
my tears disappear
in fresh-turned dirt
beneath a newly-planted tree;
saw within its wholeness,
in its evergreenness,
resurrected life,
the Christ, who lives in me,
the Christ who cares,
through me,
for broken, dying does
and newly-planted trees.

May 4, 1991